Dr. Bessie Rehwinkel

Hero of Faith

By A. Trevor Sutton

Illustrated by Linda Pierce

CONCORDIA PUBLISHING HOUSE · SAINT LOUIS

3558 S. Jefferson Ave., St. Louis, MO 63118-3968
1-800-325-3040 • www.cph.org

Written by A. Trevor Sutton
Illustrated by Linda Pierce
Edited by Rodney L. Rathmann
Assisted by Amanda G. Lansche

Manufactured in East Peoria, IL / 63692 / 160155

Table of Contents

Bessie wanted to turn around to see who it was, but she was afraid to look.

chapter one

A Young Girl's Dream

Jars and boxes of medicine, ointment, and medical supplies surrounded Bessie as she wandered around her father's office. She was not supposed to be in his office by herself, but curiosity had gotten the best of her. She studied the many interesting items resting on her father's shelves. Some jars were full of small white pills, while others held large brown pills the size of Bessie's thumb. Some of the jars were full of gooey green liquid. Others had a strange clear, foamy liquid in them.

Suddenly, something startled the curious twelve-year-old. She heard footsteps. She could tell that someone had stepped into the room. Bessie wanted to turn around to see who it was, but she was afraid to look. After all, she knew that she was not supposed be in the office alone. The footsteps came closer and closer. Finally, she felt the warmth of a hand placed on her small shoulder.

Looking up, Bessie turned around to meet its owner. She was relieved to see a familiar figure—her father —smiling at her.

Her father pulled her in for a big hug and kissed her on the forehead. He kindly reminded Bessie that she was not supposed to be in his office by herself, but his big smile told her he was willing her overlook her act of disobedience. Bessie's father was a doctor in the small town of Pierson, Iowa. He had many important tools and medicines in his office. Ever since she was very young, Bessie was always interested in what her father did in his office. She loved to watch him doing his work. In the late 1800s, when Bessie was a little girl, her family did not have electricity, so she would help her father by holding a kerosene lamp to provide light for him as he cleaned up a patient's wound. Sometimes, he let her hold the bandages as he tended the injuries of cowboys.

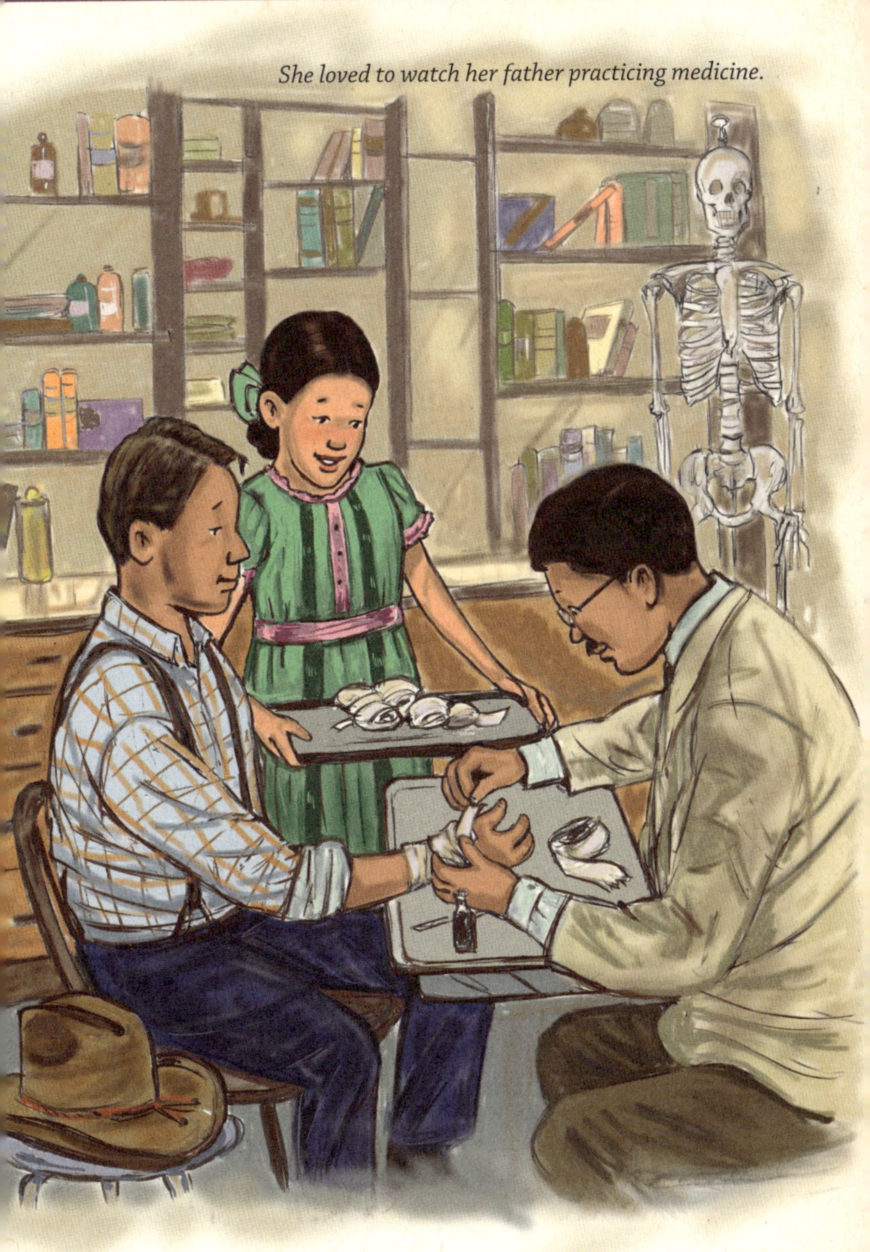

She loved to watch her father practicing medicine.

Bessie usually asked her father questions while he was treating his patients. She always had to know what he was doing and why he was doing it. Bessie's father picked up on her interest as she got older, and he would quiz her on what he should do next. The questions were generally easy. From time to time, he would ask, "Is it best to bandage the wound now, or should I clean it first?" Bessie always knew the answer to this one.

Sometimes, he would ask Bessie a tough question that she could not answer. Her father would say, "Bessie, should I use iodine or hydrogen peroxide on this?" These questions were the worst;

they made Bessie frustrated until she could feel her nose getting hot with anger. When Bessie could not take it any longer and she could feel tears coming, her father would kiss her on the forehead and tell her the answer.

When she was young, not knowing the answer to a medical question always bothered Bessie. However, as she grew older, something new began to bother Bessie. She had a very important question to answer. This was not one of her father's medical questions; this one was much more important. Bessie was growing up, and she had to decide what she wanted to do when she became an adult.

Bessie's mother and father knew exactly what they wanted her to do when she was an adult; they wanted their daughter to marry the son of the town's banker and become a wife and mother. He had already asked for her hand in marriage. When Bessie was young in the early 1900s, there were two options for young women: get married or find a job. The problem was that she wanted to do something that very few young women did at the time. Bessie wanted to be a doctor.

Bessie filled every spare moment with thoughts of becoming a doctor. She would lay in bed thinking about what her office would look like. In her mind, she could see her name on the wooden sign she would hang outside her doctor's office. She had dreams about safely delivering a baby, wrapping the infant up in blankets, and handing it to the smiling new mother.

These dreams always ended when Bessie woke up. In the morning, she still had to accept the fact that in Iowa in the year 1900, almost no one had ever heard of a female doctor. At that time, most doctors were only men. The idea of a female doctor was so unusual that Bessie told no one about her dreams.

Bessie always kept her dream of becoming a doctor to herself, until one day when she was talking with a friend of the family. The woman's name was Mrs. Benson and she had known Bessie since she was little.

Mrs. Benson encourages Bessie to become a doctor.

"Bessie, why don't you go to college and study medicine to become a doctor?" Mrs. Benson said.

It was as if Mrs. Benson could read Bessie's mind, or as if she had been in Bessie's dreams. Bessie did not even know how to respond; she was amazed that someone else thought it even imaginable for her to become a doctor. Mrs. Benson went on to tell her that she had heard of female doctors in the eastern states, such as New York and Pennsylvania. That was all Bessie needed—just one other person to believe that her dream was really possible. In that moment, Bessie decided that she was going to become a doctor.

The next day, Bessie worked up the courage to tell her father about her decision to go to college to study medicine. She did not know what his response would be. Maybe he would become angry. Maybe he would be proud of her. With sweaty palms and a pounding heart, Bessie told him what she wanted to do.

"Bessie, I hardly know what to say. Your plans come as a complete surprise to me. Why didn't you speak to me about this before? Do you realize what you are trying to do? I thought you were going to get married, but you cannot get married *and* study medicine too. You do realize that, in this day and age, people are not . . . *familiar* with the idea of a female doctor, right?" her father said.

Bessie apologized to her father for not telling him sooner. She told him she was aware that it would be difficult to find a husband while working as a doctor. Bessie told her father she had been praying about this for a long time, and it was where God was leading her.

Her father brought Bessie in for a big hug and kissed her on the forehead, saying, "Very well. You're old enough to know what you want to do. I'm very proud and happy to think that you want to become a doctor like me."

chapter two

Two Women in Medical School

When Bessie decided that she wanted to become a doctor, she knew one thing: she would eventually have to leave her family to go to medical school. Even though she knew that she had to leave home, she had no idea how hard it would be. Finally, she decided to attend the Sioux City School of Medicine in Sioux City, Iowa. Medical school was unlike anything Bessie had ever experienced before. The school was in a large city, the homework was very hard, and she missed home. Almost everything was going wrong, except for one thing: there was another girl in Bessie's class!

Her name was Clara McManus. Apart from Clara, all of Bessie's other classmates were boys. Clara had an amazing memory and could learn entire pages from their textbooks by heart. All throughout school, the two girls would study together. Clara could memorize facts, while Bessie could apply the facts to many different medical situations. This made them perfect study partners. Every day after class, Bessie and Clara would meet in the library to work together.

Bessie and Clara study together.

When Bessie started medical school, she had no idea how many new things she was going to learn. She thought she knew a lot about medicine from all of the time she had spent looking over her father's shoulder, but the more time she spent studying medicine with Clara, the more she realized there was still a lot she didn't know. Every new thing that she learned reminded Bessie of God's amazing work in creating the human body.

Bessie especially liked Psalm 139. Her favorite part came in verse fourteen: "I praise You, for I am fearfully and wonderfully made. Wonderful are Your works; my soul knows it very well." Every time she read the verse to herself or to Clara, Bessie thought about how God made people and all of the

new things she was learning about the human body in medical school.

The four years that Bessie spent with Clara and her other classmates at medical school went by quickly—almost too quickly. Graduation day arrived, and Bessie's heart was aflutter with happiness and anticipation. She was overjoyed to have achieved her childhood dream—she was finally a doctor! Still, part of her was afraid; she knew that after graduation she would have to move to a new town and open up her office. It would not be easy for her as a female doctor coming into a town that had always had male doctors. Before Bessie could think for too long about what was ahead for her, it was time to line up for the graduation ceremony.

All the families of the graduates had come for the ceremony. Bessie and her classmates, wearing robes and smiles, marched into the assembly hall. It was one of the proudest days of Bessie's life. All of her long nights studying with Clara had paid off, and she could finally put the word "Doctor" before her name.

The head teacher of the school finally said, "I now give each and every one of you the degree of Doctor of Medicine with all of its privileges, powers, and responsibilities." With those words, Bessie became Dr. Bessie Efner. With those words, her dreams became a reality!

Graduation Day

That night, as she lay in bed, a blanket of thoughts covered Bessie's mind. She was happy to finally be a doctor. She was proud of her accomplishments and proud of her friends who graduated with her. She was glad that her mother and father had come to see her graduate. Still, part of Bessie was scared. She was afraid to leave school and begin her work. She wrestled with doubt, wondering if she had what it took to go to a new place and set up shop as the first female doctor the town had ever seen. As joy mixed with nerves inside of her, Bessie did the only thing that made her feel better on nights like this. She opened her Bible and read Psalm 139 to herself. It comforted her to know that God had made her, and that He would not let her down. Bessie put down her Bible and folded her hands to pray. She thanked God for the great day she had, and she asked Him to calm her fears about beginning her new life. With a heartfelt amen, Bessie drifted off to sleep, at peace knowing she would not start her new life alone—God would always be with her.

chapter three

Doctor Bessie!

The wooden sign was nothing special. It was only roughly three feet long and about one foot high. Still, Bessie was so proud of that simple sign hanging outside her office. Bessie's father had a similar sign to designate his medical practice. Bessie loved that sign because it was proof that she had finally done what she had set out to do. She was a doctor now! She had the training, the equipment, the office, and even the sign saying that it was true. Now she lacked only one thing: patients!

Upon the advice of her father and other friends, Bessie had moved to a town in Iowa called Hinton. It was a growing farming community with many people, but no doctor. Since there was no doctor in the area, Bessie was certain that her office would be flooded with patients who needed her help. On her first day,

Bessie sat in her office waiting for any sick or injured person to knock on the door. It never happened. All day she sat around waiting, but no one came to her office. The following day, the same thing happened. During her entire first week of being a doctor, Bessie had no patients.

Bessie smiled, and again explained to the man that she was a real doctor.

Finally, that long-anticipated knock on the door came! A tall, dirt-covered farmer stood at the doorstep in a panic.

"Is the doctor in? My wife is having a baby, and I need the doctor to come to our house," the anxious farmer said.

Bessie showed him the sign that said "Dr. B. L. Efner" and explained to him that she was the doctor on the sign.

Not liking that answer, he said, "No. I mean, is the *real* doctor in? Not his helper."

Bessie smiled, and again explained to the man that she was as real of a doctor as anyone could be. Finally, left with no other option, he agreed and showed Dr. Bessie to the horse-drawn buggy that would take them to his house.

When they arrived at the house, Bessie stepped into the room where the farmer's wife was having the baby. The pregnant woman was immediately disappointed. Seeing that Bessie was a woman, she thought her husband had not found a doctor. Bessie explained to her, just like she had explained to the farmer, that she was a doctor even though she was a woman. After a few minutes, the woman relaxed and realized that Dr. Bessie was a very skilled doctor.

Bessie delivered a healthy little baby boy for the farmer's wife. As Dr. Bessie was leaving to go back to her office, the farmer's daughter stared after Bessie with wide eyes and whispered something to her father.

Bessie delivered a healthy little baby boy.

When Bessie finally got back to her office and was getting ready for bed, she had a chance to think about the day's events. She remembered that her father had told her how hard it would be working as a female doctor in a part of the country where almost no one had ever heard of such a thing. She thought about the little girl who was confused by the female doctor who delivered her baby brother. Still, Bessie was not going to let these things stop her. She had made it this far; she had finished medical school and passed all of her exams. Bessie closed her eyes and prayed that God would give her the strength and patience to deal with all of the people who doubted her. As always, Bessie concluded her prayer with a heartfelt amen as she drifted off to sleep.

The next morning, Bessie felt better about things. She was glad to have seen her first patient, and she was thankful to God for helping her deliver her first baby.

Later, Dr. Bessie was called to the bedside of a fourteen-year-old boy, the only son in a farm family. The boy suffered from pneumonia, which in the days before penicillin was often fatal. Bessie applied the best medical know-how of the day.

While the boy hung between life and death, a surprising thing happened. The boy's younger sister shyly watched Bessie at work. Later, she said to her mother, "Isn't that a funny doctor? He has no beard and wears dresses like a woman."

Thankfully, the boy recovered. The days that followed were much better for Bessie. Word spread about how she had saved the life of the farmer's son. Before long, Bessie had plenty of patients. Many women in the community preferred to have Dr. Bessie instead of a male doctor deliver their babies.

God continued to bless Bessie with more and more patients. Farmers, traveling workers, and local store owners all brought their families to Dr. Bessie's office for their health problems. Before long, no one in the town gave a second thought to Bessie being a woman; they simply thought of her as the town's doctor. Being accepted as a doctor in the community was what Bessie had wanted since she was a little girl. Things were going so well that Bessie felt she could not want anything more from life. But one day, God gave her something completely unexpected: three young girls!

chapter four
Sad Times

Tragedy struck Bessie's family in an unexpected way at the end of her first year as a doctor. Within a few months of each other, Bessie's older brother and his wife died. They had three daughters who were now without a mother or a father to take care of them. The girls—Elsie, eight years old, Ina, seven years old, and Reta, two and a half years old—loved their Aunt Bessie very much and wanted to live with her. The only problem was that Bessie did not know if she had the time or money needed to take care of the three girls. She wanted to take them into her house, but only if she could give them the care and attention they needed.

After much prayer and consideration, Bessie decided to have her three nieces live with her. She knew that she really had no other choice in the matter; she could not stand to see the girls raised by strangers.

"I have no choice. I cannot do otherwise. May the consequences be for me what they will. God will help me," Bessie thought to herself as she brought the three girls home.

Bessie brought the three girls into her home.

To Bessie's surprise, the girls were very easy to take care of. They were very thankful their Aunt Bessie had adopted them, and the girls made sure not to be a burden to her. Bessie was very pleased with her decision to adopt the girls; she realized how lonely she had been before the girls had moved in with her and how much God blessed her by bringing the children into her house. Two of Bessie's nieces would one day become nurses so that they could serve God by helping sick people get better, just like their Aunt Bessie!

Two years went by, and everything was going perfectly well for Bessie and her three nieces. Bessie had weathered the storm of losing her brother and his wife. Through it all, Bessie was blessed with three orphans that she considered her own daughters. Now, three years into being a doctor, Bessie had three girls and an ever-expanding list of patients. The year was 1906 and Bessie had moved her practice to the somewhat larger community of Moville, Iowa. Life was good for Bessie and the girls.

But then, 1907 arrived, and things changed for Bessie once again.

It was called the Panic of 1907, and it was a terrible time for many people, including Bessie and her girls. In just one year, a number of banks went out of business, and many people lost their jobs. Farmers were not able to sell their crops. People did not have enough

money to buy food, let alone pay Bessie for her medical services. Since no one had the money to pay Bessie for her work, she began to run out of money herself. She started to worry about how she would feed herself and her three nieces.

People began to move out of town to look for food and work. As more and more people left town, Bessie had fewer and fewer patients. Since a doctor needs patients to make a living, Bessie thought about packing up and leaving town with everyone else.

Bessie was out of money, out of patients, and not really sure what she should do. She decided to talk to one of her very good Christian friends about whether or not to move like everyone else.

Bessie called this friend Uncle Ira, even though he was not her uncle. Everyone in town called him Uncle Ira. He was a dear old Christian man who always went out of his way to make sure that Bessie was doing well.

Sometimes, if the light was on late in Bessie's office, Uncle Ira would knock on the door to make sure everything was all right. Bessie knew she could go to Uncle Ira for honest Christian advice about what she should do.

Uncle Ira told Bessie about an opportunity she should look into. To help all the people that had no food or work, the government was giving away free land in the western American states. At that time in American history, almost no one lived in states such as Wyoming and Montana. The government decided that if people wanted to move to those states and build cities, they would give them land for free. Uncle Ira told Bessie that many people had already taken advantage of this. As more people moved out to these western states, there was a growing need for doctors to keep everyone healthy.

As they finished talking, Uncle Ira put a one hundred dollar bill in Bessie's hand! In the early 1900s, one hundred dollars was quite a lot of money. He told her to take her three nieces and go to Wyoming. He gave her the money so that she could pay for a train ticket and move all of her belongings out West. Bessie was amazed at Uncle Ira's generosity and so glad that God had blessed her with such a great Christian friend.

As she walked home, Bessie decided to take Uncle Ira's advice. She was going to move herself and the three girls to Wyoming. She knew it would not be easy. She knew there were no big cities out West. Still, Bessie knew that God was working through Uncle Ira and the money he had given her that night. Wyoming would to be Bessie and the girls' new home.

Uncle Ira told Dr. Bessie to take her three nieces and go to Wyoming.

Bessie and the girls stepped off of the train and looked around, expecting to see the city of Carpenter.

chapter five
At Home in Wyoming

"The next stop is for passengers going to Carpenter," said the train conductor.

Bessie and the girls stepped off of the train and looked around, expecting to see the city of Carpenter. Instead of a city, they found some cows grazing next to a ranch and a small house.

Bessie followed the small group of settlers who had also gotten off the train over to the house. After explaining to the ranch owner that she was a doctor and new settler in Carpenter, she booked the ranch's spare room for the night for herself and the three girls. When she left Iowa, Bessie had made arrangements for a small house to be built on the land given to her by the government. After she and the girls spent that first night at the ranch, they would travel the short distance to their new house on the frontier.

The next morning, Bessie and the girls paid a man at the ranch to take them in a horse-drawn carriage to their land. As Bessie stepped into her new house for the first time, she suddenly knew that it was a good time to pray. A thousand thoughts crowded Bessie's mind, and she could not find the words to say a prayer. But, God knew exactly what Bessie would have liked to have said in that moment. She smiled and laughed, realizing that she had just prayed her first ever wordless prayer!

Seventy-five cents was all that Bessie had left after traveling to Wyoming and paying for their new house. Bessie trusted that God would provide for her and the girls in this new stage of her life, and God did exactly that.

Things were hard in Wyoming. Bessie and the other settlers who had moved to the western states looking for free land were called *homesteaders*. These homesteaders had left everything—their jobs, families, and friends—back East where they came from. Just like Bessie, they moved to Wyoming looking for cheap land and a better life.

Carpenter slowly grew in population. As more and more people came, the settlement began to look more like a city. There was no bank or grocery store, but there was one small church where everyone joined in worship. The church did not have an organ or a piano. Still, that did not stop the people of Carpenter from worshiping God; someone would suggest a hymn and start singing, and everyone else would simply join in!

Bessie had very few patients when she first moved West. In fact, her first patient in Carpenter was not even human—it was a sick horse! A farmer came to her office and asked Bessie to make his sick horse feel better.

Bessie's first patient in Wyoming was a horse!

Bessie explained to the farmer that she was trained in treating sick humans, not sick horses. He insisted that Bessie try to help. She gave the horse the medication that she would have given a human, and it got better! The man paid Bessie seventy-five cents for her services. With her first patient in Carpenter, Bessie doubled the amount of money she had.

Before long, Dr. Bessie had many patients—human patients—lining up in her office. She developed a very good reputation in Carpenter and people came from all over the surrounding area to have Dr. Bessie make them better. Farmers and cowboys were the most common patients in her office, but sometimes Bessie would go to people's houses to deliver babies.

One night, someone knocked on Bessie's door. When she opened it, she was stunned by what she saw. An injured young pastor stood at her doorstep.

*She had known plenty of pastors,
but none like this one.*

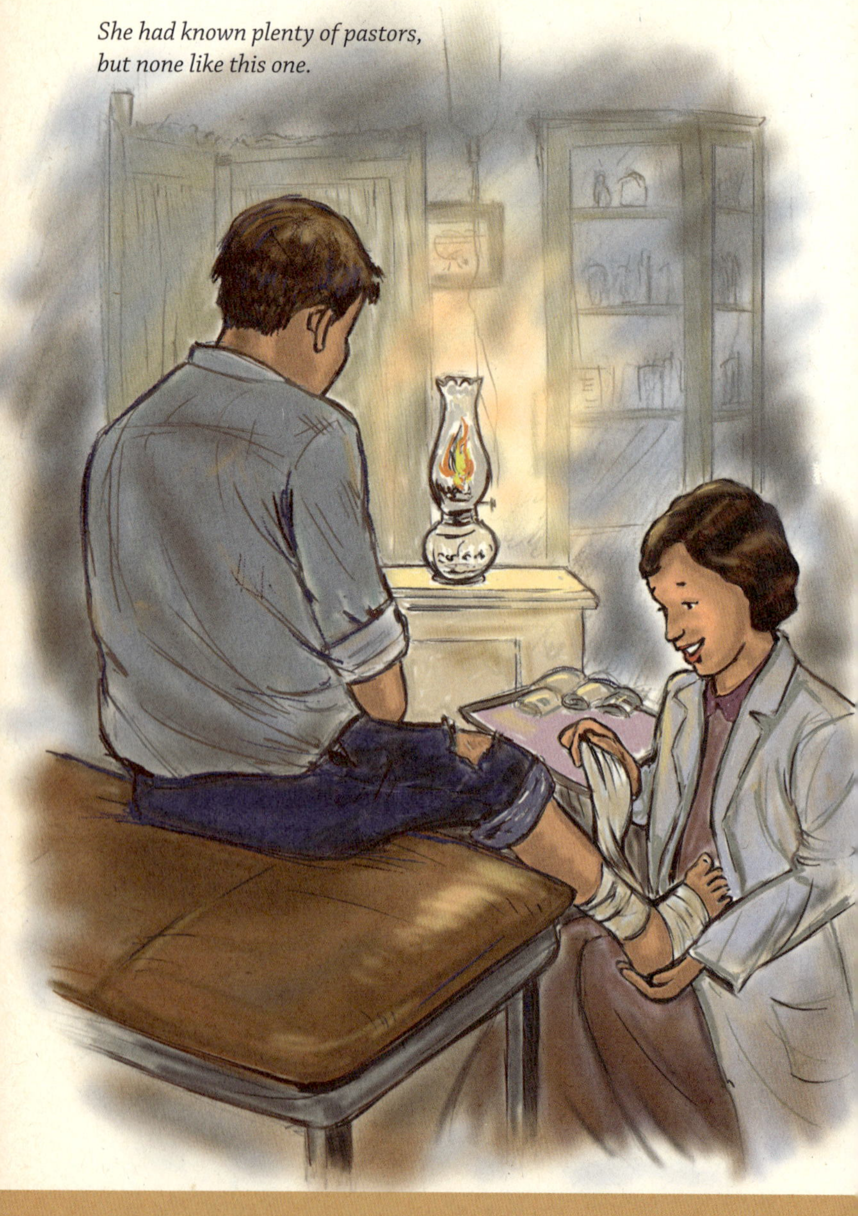

chapter six
A Pastor with an Injury

His pant leg was torn and covered in blood. Dr. Bessie burst into action and assisted the young pastor into her office. She helped him over to the operating table and asked what had happened. He was riding his horse back from a church in a different town. It was dark, and the horse accidentally walked into a wire fence. This scared the horse and it jolted forward, pinning the young pastor's leg against the wire fence and cutting it very badly in the process.

Bessie immediately went to work cleaning the young pastor's wound. She was amazed at how calm and brave this man was. The entire time she worked on his injury, he sat there politely carrying on a conversation with Bessie. She was impressed with how smart, funny, and polite he was. She had known plenty of pastors during her life, but none like this one.

She finished bandaging him and gave him some ointment to put on the cut to keep it from getting infected. After he paid Bessie what he owed and thanked her many times, the pastor told

Bessie that he really enjoyed the conversation and that he hoped to see her again. Secretly, Bessie hoped that she would see him again too.

The young pastor's hope came true; he saw Dr. Bessie again the following week. They had another very nice conversation that lasted for a few hours. Bessie found out that his name was Alfred Rehwinkel, and he was a student pastor from St. Louis, Missouri. Bessie and Alfred continued to spend time together every day for a few weeks. They would read the Bible to each other, talk about music, and tell each other stories about their childhood. Alfred would teach Bessie everything he knew about the Bible, and she would teach him about medicine. After a few months, Bessie began to really like Alfred. She thought that someday he might make a really good husband.

But, there was one problem—Alfred had to leave Wyoming to go back to St. Louis. When he left Carpenter, Bessie did not know if she would ever see him again. Alfred promised that he would faithfully write her letters while he was away. True to his word, Bessie received a letter from Alfred every two weeks. Bessie was always excited when she received one of his letters. He wrote her as often as he could, and she always responded quickly. For an entire year, they exchanged many letters.

She would see Alfred again!

One day, Bessie received a special delivery letter from Alfred, and she was curious about what the letter might be about. It said that he would be coming back soon to the western states to be a pastor in the area. She would see Alfred again! Bessie was very surprised and very happy.

When he finally came back to see her, Alfred surprised Bessie once more. He asked her if she would marry him! Bessie was overwhelmed by Alfred's question, but she immediately said yes!

Before long, in September of 1912, Bessie and Alfred were happily married. From then on, Bessie told people that if it had not been for a scared horse in Wyoming that ran into a fence, she would not be married! Once she was married to Alfred, Bessie's life changed in many ways. She changed her last name from Efner to Rehwinkel. Soon, she would move with her new husband to northwestern Canada, where she would be the wife of the pastor of several frontier churches.

chapter seven

Mrs. Rehwinkel

When she was twenty-five years old, Bessie had smiled when she heard people call her "Doctor Bessie." She was proud to be a doctor and serve God's people in that way. Now that she was married, something else made Bessie proud. Being called "Mrs. Rehwinkel" made Bessie smile and thank God for all the new blessings in her life. Now that she was married, Bessie did not work as a doctor. Her days were still filled with caring for people, just in a different way.

The Rehwinkels make a new home in Edmonton—a large cosmopolitan city.

Northwest Canada was home for the newly married Pastor Alfred and Bessie Rehwinkel. When they first moved to Canada, Alfred served small churches on the frontier. Bessie did not mind this at all, because it reminded her of when she lived in Wyoming. The people on the Canadian frontier were homesteaders just like the people on the western frontier of the United States. Still, Bessie preferred Canada for one reason—she was able to share her life with Alfred!

After only about a year and a half on the Canadian frontier, Alfred received an important letter telling him that he was needed at a church in the large Canadian city of Edmonton. As faithful servants to God's Church, Bessie and Alfred packed their belongings and moved to Edmonton.

Edmonton was unlike anywhere Bessie had ever been. It was a very large city with many people from many different countries. Immigrants from all over the world came to live in Edmonton. With all of the immigrants living in the city, Bessie constantly learned new things; never before had she heard so many different languages and eaten so many different types of foreign foods.

Alfred was the pastor of St. Peter's Lutheran Church in Edmonton, Canada, for fourteen years. Pastor Alfred worked hard to make sure all of the immigrants at his church felt welcomed in their new country. Together, Alfred and Bessie made sure the immigrants had somewhere to work and a school for their children to attend.

During their fourteen years in Edmonton, something very exciting happened for the Rehwinkel family: Bessie and Alfred had three children! They first had a girl named Dorothy. She was followed by another girl named Helen. Finally, they had a boy named Eugene. Both Dorothy and Helen grew up and became nurses so they could serve God's people like their mother. Eugene grew up and became a pastor so he could serve God's people like his father.

Bessie and Alfred had three children!

After sixteen years in Canada, Alfred received another important and unexpected letter. The letter asked him if he would come back to the United States to be the president of St. John's, a Lutheran college in Winfield, Kansas! After reading the letter to Bessie, they both decided that before anything else, they should pray. By the time they said amen, Bessie and Alfred looked at each other and knew that God was calling them to go back to the United States!

Soon, the Rehwinkel family had left Canada for another new home. Bessie was glad to be in Kansas for many reasons, but one in particular made her very happy—she got to work once more as a doctor! The college had asked Bessie if she would serve as the school's doctor. She gladly agreed, happy to be serving God's people in this way once again.

Bessie was invited to help the doctors at two different hospitals in the area. She would meet with these doctors and talk with them about their interesting and challenging cases. It felt good to be practicing medicine again. While living in Canada, Bessie had not had time to work as a doctor. She kept busy with her duties as a mother and a pastor's wife. Now that her children were grown up and Alfred was the president of a college, Bessie could go back to being Dr. Bessie!

After eight years in Winfield, Kansas, Alfred Rehwinkel received a special delivery letter. This

Bessie and Alfred at Concordia Seminary in St. Louis, Missouri.

letter was from Concordia Seminary in St. Louis, Missouri. Alfred had attended Concordia Seminary as a student before he met Bessie.

The letter asked if he would become a professor at the seminary in St. Louis. As they always did, Bessie, Alfred, and the children gathered together and prayed that God would let them know what He wanted them to do. As usual, by the time the family said amen, they knew that God was calling them to go. The Rehwinkel's packed their bags and moved to Missouri.

Bessie and Alfred spent the remainder of their lives in St. Louis, Missouri. Alfred served God's people as a seminary professor, teaching young men how to serve the church in their callings as pastors. Bessie and Alfred enjoyed walking around the campus of the seminary in the evening hours. They loved to admire the beautiful campus and marvel at the intricacies of God's creation.

Bessie was now eighty years old. She loved to sit under one of the many large oak trees at the seminary, watch the sun slip below the horizon, and think about how God had blessed her. She would think about her life when she was a young, single woman working as a doctor and raising her nieces on the rough and unforgiving Wyoming frontier. She would think about how a wild Wyoming horse brought an injured young pastor to her office, and how he later became her husband. She would think about her time in the diverse city of Edmonton and her three children. She would think of her time in Kansas as the wife of a college president and finally, of her years on the campus of the seminary in St. Louis.

Often, when Bessie thought about her life, Psalm 23 was on her lips. Bessie would say, "The Lord is my shepherd" with an enormous smile. She knew that although she had lived in many places, God remained with her. Bessie's life was always in God's hands—and that was where she always wanted to be!

Bessie's life had always been in God's hands!

Timeline of Events
during Dr. Bessie Rehwinkel's Life

1873 Bessie Efner born in Galesburg, Iowa on March 28

1876 Custer defeated at Battle of Little Big Horn

1879 Women lawyers permitted to argue cases before the Supreme Court

1903 The Wright brothers make their first flight

1907 The Panic of 1907; Dr. Bessie moves to Wyoming as a homesteader

1908 General Electric patents electric toaster

1912 Dr. Bessie Efner and Rev. Alfred Rehwinkel marry and move to Canada

1914 Rehwinkels move to Edmonton, Alberta, Canada; World War I begins

1917 Russian Revolution; USSR formed

1919 World War I ends with Treaty of Versailles

1920 Nineteenth Amendment is passed, giving women the right to vote

1927 Lindbergh flies non-stop across the Atlantic

1928 Rehwinkels move to Winfield, Kansas

1929 Stock market crashes; Great Depression begins

1936 Rehwinkels move to St. Louis; Alfred becomes a professor at Concordia Seminary

1939 Germany invades Poland; World War II begins

1941 United States enters World War II

1945 World War II ends

1957 Soviets launch Sputnik, the world's first artificial satellite put into Earth's orbit

1962 Bessie Rehwinkel dies on May 26